An Art Form

The Crass Poetry Collection

Jeremy Void

Other books by Jeremy Void

Derelict America
short stories and essays

Nefarious Endeavors
short stories and some poetry

Smash a Lightbulb:
Poetry for Lowlifes
poetry, prose, creative essays, and more

Erase Your Face:
The SkullFuck Collection
visual poetry

Just a Kid
experimental prose and poetry

Sex Drugs & Violence:
Incomplete Stories for the Incomplete Human
incomplete stories

www.chaoswriting.net

An Art Form

THE CRASS POETRY COLLECTION

Jeremy Void

An Art Form: The Crass Poetry Collection

ISBN Number:
978-0-578-16638-4

ChaosWriting Press

IT'S A MINDFUCK
www.chaoswriting.net

To Chuck
a.k.a.
"De-Chuck-Tive"

To the police

To all the enemies I've acquired over the years

To all those who have tried to silence me

Preface

This book did not come from a place of anger.

I'm not an angry person.

I am a mere poet and a Punk rocker, and I like fast music and blunt poetry.

If you don't like it, good, because it doesn't like you.

I admit, however, that I do have sick demons inside me, just aching to come out. But don't we all?

I use my poetry as a way for me to cope with the wrath of my demons, as opposed to bottling them up inside and allowing them to torment me till the end of time.

This is my third book of poetry.

I call it "The Crass Poetry Collection" because it is quite crass; I wanted to go back to my roots, rooted in Punk rock and destruction, angst and frustration for the lonely boy wasting away his days in class, a ticking time bomb—*tick tick tick*—stewing in his own fucked-up madness, and I wanted to write a book specifically for that....

A book that speaks to the sick generation—the boys and girls fed up with conventions and standards.

That said, I hope you enjoy this book.

Table of Discontents

acceptance

went to a party last night.
got the cold shoulder by
the first 3 or 4 i tried
to talk to, so i sat alone, in a chair,
pulled out my book,
& the moment i started reading it,
an older woman appeared before me,
reaching past me & retrieving
her purse which sat alone beside me—
my only company taken away,
for she probly thought id snatch it up
& take all her cash.

truth be told, i didnt even see it there
didnt even care.
jus wanted to sit in peace
& read my book—alone & alone
the way it was meant to be
.... but no, im a common crook
me, w/ my tight black jeans,
long shaggy hair & holy shirt i wore
ruffled & dirty. why me?

because thats the way
its meant to be—
forever & ever & ever.

doomed to a life of solitude,
i walk the streets & keep my head
down trying to do my own thing
.... but no, not me.
it will never happen any other way
not even in my wildest dreams.

sometimes

sometimes i act real crazy
but i can assure you my heart
is always there, it always beats
& throbs as i pass thru the
bloody rainbow into your mind.

sometimes i want to unwind,
but i cant find it, the answer is blind.
sometimes my mind races.
it races & i get restless & pace.

my brain beats like a heart,
pumping knowledge into me like
im receiving a reverse lobotomy.
i dont know why that happens why its
the case except that it happens
& my brains melts into ashes.

i know you think that im weird.
did i tell you i can read your mind?
i know you think that im strange.
did i tell you that i am in fact

deranged .... so much its like
im my own mother & father having
conceived me when i was a toddler.

i sometimes live as fast as
a runaway freight train robbed by
gangster cowboys w/ hatchets.
other times my life moves like a
snail squirming along as it
wins the race. those times
when im the slowest are the times
when i feel the farthest left behind.
i feel like ive gotta catch up
because if i dont the world
will explode & itll all be
my fault.

i wudnt be able to live
w/ myself in the absence of
reality the real world everything
youve come to know & luv but
which ive come to know & despise.
all of that crap i know now is so utterly
important & yet i wish for it to
be nuked like apple pie. be eaten
like a chimpanzee eats maggots off
the dead flesh of a fallen beast
in the wild west & you know
exactly what im saying only
im sure you really dont.

youre as lost as i am
probly so now ive gotta cry....

day in day out

day in day out we
kicked life in the balls
spat in its face—
day in day out.

we rode the bull till the bull
bit dirt, then we dismounted
& kicked it in the head
punched it in the face until
blood spurted & pooled beneath
its head.

on the subway, in back alleys, atop
bridges & underneath the railroad tracks
we ran & frolicked in our own filth,
creating more filth for the yuppie class to
clean up. we did it all, knocking back &
cracking skulls, hopping pogoing flailing
& divebombing till the last mans dead.

life is a beast, a great big fuckin beast
that we maimed w/ a two-by-four, speared it

w/ our own fists, & pelted it w/
our steel-toed boots. blood splattering in
our toothless faces—& we smiled amid
the gore. our grins sick & freakish.
wide & missing teeth.

like bonnie & clyde, we robbed the yuppies
blind, big businesses cringed at all the mischief
we stirred, the hell we conjured up & blasted
in their faces.

thats right, you & me babe, we
delivered fierce stabs, stabbing the outsiders
in their backs, necks, & faces, piercing their hearts
w/ our own spiked tongues.

we did it all, day in day out,
& then we went home

& went to bed.

evolution

im slowly learning the ways
of the world, like i was born jus yesterday
& growing older at a rapid rate.
every event, every moment, every
failed effort, every successful endeavor—
it all adds up until one day
soon i hope
i gain control of my own fate
& i no longer haveta rely on others
to take me there. but on my own accord
i can rise above the ranks & be so much
better than the man i was the day before.

doom

the inevitable looms
ahead of me like a
stop sign but i do not
yield. i keep pushing forward.

a king lost in his own castle

im an outcast among outcasts.
i stand out in a crowd made up
of flamboyant outfits & colored hair.
im a freak among freaks, too
freakish to fit in here, too
freakish to fit in there….
but then, i dont care because
im used to being ill fit, used to being the pun
of gods sick joke, of your cruel classifications
that smack me w/ ironic labels—its ironic,
isnt it?

i have no place in this phony world
a punk from the 1970s born in
the wrong era the wrong time
& ill tell you for me living equals suicide.

only one way out i know which is death
death death death, by whose hand exactly?
mine or the systems?

im a loser among losers.

im bold & blunt, & yes i might
be too blunt even for this crowd.
they cringe when i read my poetry.
they look away & leave the room
as if what i haveta say is gratuitous & they
simply have no time for it—that or theyre
absolutely appalled by the truth.

the unspun truth, the bluntest blow
a livid excuse if there ever was one
seeking an alibi to sneak away & not hear
what i haveta say. its sad *and* its true
but you know what?

you can shit on me & call me names.
you can walk away & pretend
i dont exist. well you know what?

fuuuuuuck you!!!! thats the end of
that.

a poem for richard hell

i first bought your album when i was
19
        blank generation
it was a self-birthday present, a day or two
before chuck came & picked me up
& took me to the cape to go camping
w/ my girlfriend.

we listened to your album most the ride
interrupted by the endless laughter
that banged & splashed in the confines
of his pickup truck.

right away i fell madly in luv w/
your poetic lines, your ability to
explain the unexplainable in a way
that i cud relate to.
i felt in fact like you & i might be
soulmates.

i remember dancing in the parking lot to
down at the rock & roll club

Jeremy Void

while we waited for our dealer to deliver
us a bag of coke so we cud shoot it
at the gorgeous prostitutes place.

we danced & we laughed, while
downtown at dawn reverberated in
the background. it played as the
soundtrack to every lost boy & girl
roaming the city streets—
                    & i was lost.

when i went to treatment in vermont,
i read your novel, *go now,* & it
blew me away—the first full novel i ever
read & im glad that i did.

i have video footage of me & friends
blowing lines atop your book *hot and cold,*
which happened to be the first book i
ever owned.

you gave me music to kill the boredom
w/, music i cud get high to
& dance to
& sit around & listen to
fast & witty, quick & sentimental,
w/ that old school punk rock beat.

you gave me poetry i cud recover to.
i searched the internet for your contact info
to tell you that your written work saved
my fuckin life.

a jigsaw porcupine

when you wake up in the morning
& your head feels weighted down
& you cant find a spot to piss amid
all the sleeping bodies splayed out on
the basement floor, you know somethings
gotta give & its gotta give quick.
you spend day in & day out
partying it up w/ punk rock people
going to shows & moshing till you jus
dont know anymore. the music is
too fast for your old age sinking in, &
your eardrums burst—& you panic.
all of this coming to you at the show when
youre dancing & having a blast.
you ignore the premonition & continue to
flail & swing until somebody crashes
into you & knocks you into the amp
looming over the crowd, the amp breaks & falls.
the lights go out, youre waking up on the moon
& theres others like you on this space shuttle.
your teeth grind as you try to remember
you try to remember

you try to remember, but your vain attempts
at recapturing the past seem quite futile
& instead you sit in the corner & brood
about it.

you analyze your life
put it under the microscope & figure
out the things that make you tick.
you scratch your dick while you await
results. the slip of paper streaming outta
the printer shows you
nothing
a blank slate—& you wonder how
that cud be,
for after all you *know* you are
clinically insane & the behaviors of your
past prove it all the same.
you stare at the blank slate
at the nothingness & wonder
why the world spins & why you cant
make it spin the other way. i wud luv
to rotate the world, make time go in
reverse, but fates got another plan & you
my friend are already dead.

another day goes by.
i have plans big plans to get out
of this rut but time it moves too fast
to understand & soon ill be 80-years
old in a rocking chair complaining that
i didnt act fast enough

all these regrets, like tadpoles swimming
around my conscious, all this remorse burning
me up like my head is on fire, & you wonder
how you lived to be so old. you shud have died
years ago you know, but fates got its own plan
& this plan is unpredictable & what makes
sense has no sense to speak of.

i listen to my heart beat
i listen to the clicking of my fingers
as they tap & press keys on the keyboard
as i type this poem in hyper-speed.
your heart tells me to stop that hurts
my heart tells me to proceed that hurts.
pain is a figment of our imagination & some of us
enjoy it & some of us dont.
you my friend are in the class of the painlessly
driven the hopelessly devoted, the lost few
who suffer terrible migraines that rob us of our youth.
lets see, a description of something—well, ill describe
my pain when it tears thru my lungs & wobbles
like dominos dipped in blood. i watch as snakes slither
thru the garden & their forked tongues slip out
of their mouths, sizzling as it grasps for
the child playing in the sand box.
the parents dont notice the snake there, & it creeps
into the yard & gobbles down the child like its a
giant mouse.

but heres the thing,
the snake is not a snake at all.

its a serpent big enough to make you hovel in fear
make you crawl & search endlessly for the ball.
but the ball is spiked, & the punch they serve is
like a virgins cherry, so sweet its almost sensual.
raw but innocent ready to lose its innocence to a
fat man in an overcoat walking w/ giant feet that
clomp on the sidewalk, *clomp clomp clomp*
hes a giant.

your life flashes once, twice, three times,
before your eyes, & the sight of such a
wasted existence makes you hate yourself even more.
you reach up to claw out your own eyeballs to stop
the images from taking shape cuz you jus cant
accept the truth even if it came in the form of a fat man
in an overcoat wearing military boots who stomped
clomped
whomped
your bare foot w/ the heel of his polished boot—
thats the truth thats why they say
the truth hurts, because itll wind up its arm
like a pitcher at a baseball game, & when its
back as far as it can go, itll send its arm
thru the air like a dart honing in on its target
& the truth will knock you on your ass.

thats why its not safe
to mess w/ the fuckin gnomes!

faster/slower

faster faster faster
thats what theyd say
when their life zips thru existence
like a laser beam.

slower slower slower
thats what theyd say
when theyre walking thru a minefield
that their fast-paced life had led them to
              in the first place.

on dreaming

sometimes i dream of things. big things, sometimes small, but mostly big & unobtainable, out of reach for the likes of me. i guess i dont dream as much as i used to, now that i think about it. (when i say dream, I mean *fantasy*, by the way.) i cant remember the last real dream (fantasy) i had—cant remember what it was about. maybe that means ive lowered my expectations some. i mean, i used to be a bit of an idealist, always in an existential (dressed-up nihilism) funk. it really got me down. you see, i claimed to be a nihilist—only i always pronounced the word wrong even tho i *knew* the actual pronunciation (i dont believe in pronouncing words properly, id say—pure nihilism—because id grown up pronouncing it this way (niy-ilism) my whole life & i wasnt gonna change for nobody)—but i cud never accept that there was nothing beyond the scope of vision. there is nothing, i know now, or maybe theres something, i dont know—either way the answers i seek are too dense for my finite brain to compre-hend, so i jus leave it like that: it is what it is, it was what it was, the past is carved in stone, cant be changed by anyone, especially not by me, & the future is a mystery waiting to be revealed. if only i had foresight, cud somehow see the future. if i had super powers. or even if i jus had access to money that cud afford all that i need & then some & then maybe i cud buy my girl a nice leather jacket for halloween. she/d put it on, id wrap my arms around her, & instantly we/d float up up up & up, straight up until we/re airborne, flying thru the dark, cloudy sky like two super heroes in luv. see what i mean? & then id work myself into a fit when reality snaps back in & id crack my chin on the stone cold existence that is my life: a baby brought into this world for gods own sick enjoyment—wait, i thought we established there is no god; either way there might be some form of deity in the clouds watching over us, & the day—morning, afternoon, or evening; one or the other—i weaseled my way outta my mothers womb & took my first whiff of pure air, the deity, eyes insanely wide, jaw suddenly dropping, tongue hanging loose & sloppy in its shapeless maw, a rumble growing in its gut, stirring fierce & frightening, surging up into its chest, past where its heart wud be if only it were human, up thru its throat, & exploding from its mouth in cackling hysteria, died of laughter—the deity died that day, god is dead, faith is dead, & i fuckin killed it & now ive gotta live w/ that, w/ all the knowledge that i damned the human race to hell, if such a thing even exists in the first place. i mean, dont get me wrong, im not exactly anybody special or anything; im jus another bozo on the bus, as they say, along for the ride. really, that whole bit about me killing god is jus another one of my dreams—or moreover, nightmares. like i said, i havent had a legitimate dream in years; but this godforsaken brain of mine, it doesnt ever stop. its like an endless film reel spurning out a travesty of situations that i can easily project into the real world, & sometimes, if not most of the time, these projections really get me down, so i try not to think about it. i let the nightmares churn deep in my sub-conscious & i dont try to fight it, because when i jus let it happen & maybe laugh about it later, these torturous images dont seem to carry as much weight & i can easily brush them away w/ a simple

flick of my wrist. they come & go & i dont know, i guess ive come
to luv my lack of dreams & my knack for horribly visceral night-
mares that pray on me when im asleep at night. i wudnt trade
them for anything. because after all, dreams make me feel worst.
wake up from a wonderful dream & where are you? how do you
feel now? now that your fantasy has faded away & reality sets in
harder than ever like a haymaker punch straight to your face. but
wake up from a terrible nightmare, & boy, am i so glad to be back
home....

change

change change change
we/re constantly changing
& i fuckin hate change.
wheres the reset button,
restart ive made a mistake.
i wanna do it again i wanna start
from square one & do it
one more time jus one more time.

but
it
wont
ever
stop.

my heartbeat quickens.
my pulse spikes.
the baby grows older
& i feel like a toddler.
whered the time go....

oh no i hold on for

my dear life but the boat it
rocks & the earth it turns.
the car runs a red light
speeding outta control.

stop stop stop, tap tap tap
the man is speaking my eyes
are tweaking
as i search the streets for some
speed speed speed.

change change change
the word is churning & one day
the sun will explode.
but not in my lifetime they say because
ill be dead & gone before the world
ends before it burns down before
the zombies rize up from the ground—
an apocalypse is
among us & its changing
but i fuckin hate change.
change change change

why wont it stop?...

Q me in

i sit in my hell
waiting for fate to sweep me away..
its a deep swim
a big swim
an epic emersion of waves that
come up swirling & sucking like
a fuckin vacuum taking me out.
i wait for the day to end.
i wait for the week to end.
oh when will this month end?
the year has only jus begun
& the seasons are harsh & right
ripe & in charge
so stark i can barely see whats ahead
of me & i wonder how itll end.

will it end?
or will i go on living
forever & ever, now
thats my biggest fear:
eternal life—get me outta here.
if i dont get out soon, ill

lose it that climb is high too high to climb
& im scared of what it holds &
if ill ever get there alive. if ill survive
the hailstorm in my mind, like fuckin
seizurish hurricanes rocking the world
like evaporating tsunamis coming down
& taking out & knocking down the walls
that for so long ive held up so strong.

but then, that bores me.
the thinking of it bores me
& i like to be alone & awake
when the dawn comes to my world
& says *why dont you come w/ me*
> *ill take you away from here, honey*
> *youll see, as the world sleeps, life*
> *(life / death)*
> *(life / death)*
> *it will come & please you, as*
> *sweet as honey, youll See.*

i admit im rather weary at first.
but the night can be quite sneaky
& it wisps me away on its magical cords.
the greatest trick the night ever pulled
was convincing the world to sleep while
it overtakes the earth & crimelords roam
freely & rob & kill simply because they can
because its time its time
for the mayhem & i want some action
some fuckin action, enough to get me off.

Q me in

i wanna ride a pony, w/ a sack of drugs wrapped over
the saddle, & i wanna deliver said drugs
to junkies who will OD & die the night of—

now, wudnt that be fun?

killing the silence

I CANT STAND silence.
i fill the gaps w/ VIOLENCE—

senseless acts to fill the gaps
that make me mad w/ rage.
i hate the nothingness that
roils when nothing is going down.
im bleeding cant you see
my heart gushing thick red streams.
i bleed because theres not a thing
to do in this boring old town.
its a rut i tell you, a fuckin rut
that bores me to fuckin death.
the only thing left for me to do
is beat my head against this red brick wall.
ill beat it till i fall.

restless & bored

one of these days
ill rip out my hair.
one of these days
i might jus die.
im going nowhere, sitting here,
restless & bored
    restless & bored
        restless & bored
restless & so utterly bored.
my mind spiraling in a void,
devoid of anything worthwhile.
i wonder oh how i wonder.
my thoughts put me
to sleep.
i think oh how i think
about nothing at all.
NO t h i n g.
i
am
so fuckin
bored…. bored & bored
& getting boreder.

aaaaaaaaah....
look for me
in the obituaries because
im bored to fuckin
death.

darkness

another cigarette smoked.
another cup of coffee drunk.
i sit in the dark as my mind
races like a racecar dashing
my hands trembling faster.
the coffee cup jingles in my
jittery hands.
another day spent.
another day lost.
a maddening worry erupting inside
me like a racking pain thrumming deep
deep
deep
deep in my sub-conscience.
the tv showing static.
the sound buzzing like a
pack of bumble bees.
i hate the sound but i
let it play regardless because
its much better than that....

that which will kill me.

just a rant

THIS IS JUST A RANT
THIS IS JUST A RANT
IF YOU LOOK TOO DEEPLY INTO
ANYTHING I SAY I WILL SURELY
MAKE YOU PAY
       the hard way....

    another morning.
    another reason to feel bored.
    another hopeless yearning as i
    wish to the sky & ask for something
    to change....
    anything in fact—jus one nudge
    budging my life outta this
    hole ive spent day in & day out
    burrowing into.

    im 27-years old, going on
    28 & i feel like a geezer writing
    another sappy poem about nothing.
    i peaked in my teens & kept going
    when i reached 20 & you bet i was

just a rant

thru the roof at 21, headless in massachusetts
brainless in boston, drunk all day
& night & the hangover never came
because i was drunk all the time—
        all the F-ing time (i figure
                now im much too old to swear,
ive gotta learn to mature & grow
outta these words cuz im an adult now)
                ——*YAAAAAAWN!!!!*

i never wanted to grow up
never wanted to be here in vermont
never wanted to be an adult child
who hangs out w/ kids so much younger
than him because ive gotta relive those days
vicariously.

i never wanted any of that.
but now ive got it & its a bright spring
morning only god skipped over the spring & said
HEY HEY, FUCK YOUR SPRING, HERES SUMMER.
the days are blazing hot & the nights, tho cooler,
make me sweat like no other, sweat gushing
down my slick slick skin. oily & grotesque
as a result of all the moronic stress i face on
a day to day basis. that or i havent bathed in a week.

last night i finished editing *Nefarious Endeavors*
        the second edition
sent out for another ISBN & im psyched to get it
only the waiting, the patience it takes, is so irritating

that i sit here & fiddle w/ my dick because theres
not much else i can do about it in the meantime
except wait
    — & wait —
        — & wait —
            — & wait —
only I really really hate things that make
me wait, so much its like i despise anyone
who gets in my way. i wanna knock em down
& hock loogies on their fallen bodies—now
wudnt that be fun?...... a hocking loogy party
where we/d gather around a fallen person &
suck back air to capture the phlegm in our throats,
making a grotesque snort that stuckup girls will run
from when they hear it, a snort that to me sounds rather neat,
& fuck em if they cant take a joke. & we stand
around & spit the balls of phlegm on the fallen
man or woman—either one works—who takes it like
a champ squirming & yelping & holding up
hands to block the plummeting wads of snot—sounds
like a brilliant plan.

have you ever met anyone whose ideas
are all really terrible ideas clothed in a quick-
paced energy needed to pull them off in the first place?
well thats me; thats exactly the kinda person i am.
im Jeremy Void, the man w/ a plan whose ideas jus
plain suck but ill rub em in your face like theyre
made of mud, smear your lips & smother your eyes
jus so i can get my kicks, you know you know you know

just a rant

THIS IS JUST A RANT
THIS IS JUST A RANT
IT SHOULD BE TREATED AS SUCH
OR ELSE YOU MIGHT WAKE UP
       dead....

pretty bitch

i hate you.
youre a pretty snob
a pretty bitch
rich & pretty &
i fuckin hate your kind.

self-sabotage

alone.

going nowhere.

i get what i want,
but im jus gonna lose it anyway.
its a futile struggle, a lost
battle, a war going on in my head.
my eyes flick here & there as i search
for a distraction, i search
for validation, i search for someone
anyone
jus one fuckin person

to tell me that im worthless.

i bob & toss & turn.
i sweat & i pant.
the clock ticks relentlessly.
its an endless struggle
an existential hustle.
i dont care anymore.

i kick a hole in the wall.
i take some drugs & try
to sit down & forget
it all, but the facts keep
coming back up. like a drowning man
refusing to stay down.

the black spraypaint traverses the white wall.
my head hurts so i bash it some more & start
to bleed leaving splotches of red amid the lines of black.
a deep, unsettling chuckle leaves me like a
humorous hiccup & i know i will never be able
to return the bridge is burned & i can never
come back.

good riddance.

bound to happen anyway....

rebel rebel

i stare at the crowd.
they all look the same to me.
since when did rebellion
become cool? since when did
it hit the social scene?
is dressing like a rebel really
rebelling when everyones

doing it?

im a freak, yes thats true.
you might think im a mongoloid too.
to you im weird & you veer the other way
every chance you can get, jus evade
me like im carrying a bucket filled w/
agent orange like you might catch my
leprosy if you come anywhere near me.

but heres the thing: i keep on keeping on
doing my own thing, breaking the
rules i dont approve of & obeying
the ones that i do. & youre the rebel?

keep on hanging out w/ the crowd.
itll get you nowhere
but to a black hole, spiraling into a void
that materialized out of your own filthy existence.
be a rebel, if thats what you are.
be a rebel, if thats what you want.
         hey, its what everyone else is doing,
           right?
           so why not? right?

drink your fuckin koolaide & die.

                <<~~   ~~~   ~~>>

to me all i wanna be
all ive ever wanted to be in this boring old
       life of mine
is jus one simple thing:

i want to be me....

shunned & ignored

im so sick of going to the bar
to the open-mike
& seeing a young girl whod seen me read
before walk out the moment i start.
im so sick of the evil eyes i get
for being a mere human, a good person.
im so sick of the looks i get when
i walk into the coffee shop & order myself
a drink. i want a drink....

i get real irritated when im not
given a measly chance
when im profiled
judged
thrown to the wolves.
at least the wolves dont judge me

cuz everybody else, they toss around labels
like its spare change, dropping it into
the poor mans cup. as long as the lid goes on.

get me out of this world where girls

are so high & mighty they stare down from
their plateaus like theyre lions
like theyre fuckin lions
well im the lion hunter & im slinging
my net in their directions.

im so tired of the people in this town
pedestal people thinking they know better
like theyre the doctor ready to diagnose
me w/ sick symptoms to make themselves
look good feel good—feel better than me.

well, youre not better than me.

it really irks me when im observed
by the mass public, pisses me off
to be watched by them, by the retarded class

who get brained senseless by the relentless
amounts of television they watch.
who lose themselves in reality tv shows
real (fake) people in real (fake) situations—
& these are the people who look down at me.

beady eyes & upturned noses
sneers & standoffish poses
i want none of what theyre selling
& yet it bothers me to no end
that these people think theyre better
than me..................... cut your fuckin
wrists in the fuckin bathtub drown on
your own motherfuckin blood.

god forbid

the truth hurts & god forbid
i describe you w/ my words.

pre-disappointment

i wait for something big,
but i know itll never come.
i swing my fists & kick my legs,
cursing the fate that has yet to come.

im disappointed again.
another let-down has got me again.
i dream big & my hopes explode,
a flurry of energy that defuses like a gush of water
smothering an epic fire.

i sit & i wait,
but the efforts go unnoticed.
im impatient & restless,
my thoughts spinning a travesty of
projections that make me depressed,
my imagination burning me up like wildfire,
scenarios bouncing off my skull like a game of pong.

i hope for the best but expect the worst
& yet my fate seems to have a plan of its own

& i cant escape it
no matter how far i go.

looking down thru your nose

im the little man that
you spit upon.
im trash to you, a bonified loser
nobody cares for because my ideas
are tripe & my ways are so foreign
to you that you can smother me &
nobody will care.

im a human & i have jus as much
a right as any of you. ive got a voice
& ill use my voice & if youve got
a problem w/ that then thats your problem
        not mine,
            so keep that in mind….

so next time you try to silence me for the greater good
or whatever you wanna call it to justify your botch reasoning,
jus remember this—remember that ive got
an equal right to be here & to speak.

i disagree w/ where you stand but
i let you stand there because you have that right.

but i have the right to stand here
     to spit
     to swear
     to raise my middle finger
in the air.

keep it in mind that next time
you climb onto your high horse &
look down at me—that you & i

are no different in the end.

we both bleed red. we/re two humans
w/ differing sets of values but
we/re still human in the end & we were born into the same
     race—
the human race....

a hot date

ive got a hot date tonight
only she didnt show.
anyone wanna take her place?

& & &

i stare in the mirror
i stare in the mirror & wonder
i stare in the mirror i hate
i stare in the mirror the mirror mocks
mocks me mocks me

i listen to the song
i listen to the song skip
it skips & pops & i realize
id much rather stare in the mirror
for one minute longer.

i stare out the window
nothing happens out there
a dog eats a squirrel
i stare out the window &

taking a piss now & watching
i piss & watch the pee hit the water
the yellow water swirls & splashes
in the next room plays that same damn song

skipping & popping like a ruined record

i eat breakfast now, & the
i eat pancakes & eggs
it tastes like crap but its all
i stab the pancakes w/ the fork
shovel it in my mouth & gag

i dread the day to come
sitting in a cubicle isnt very fun
dont worry about what the ads say
sitting in a cubicle is lame as shit

i stare in the mirror
i watch myself blink blink blink
nothing like watching your lids flicker
i stare in the mirror & & &

a bird tweets somewhere outside
i slam the window shut to block the
my cat rubs against me it feels soft & purrs
it feels like a pillow & reminds me of sleep

i stare in the mirror
i stare in the mirror i dont
i wear a blue suit w/ no
i wear a tie that makes me think
about things, like

i wonder what wud happen if
i hanged myself w/ it.

Jeremy Void

i stare in the mirror & & &
i cant take it anymore
i hurl my fist at the mirror
the mirror explodes & glass
i sit on the floor & frolic in the shards
they cut my skin but thats okay....

the twilight zone

its hard to stay miserable when everything—
life
people
circumstances
the works
—is going right in your life, & i find it hard
to write when thats the case.

its like
i never thought things wud
turn around like this.
its like
i jus didnt expect it
you know.
not like this, anyway....
its like
im a sick person & i dont deserve
this kind of outcome. i dont deserve
this kind of life.
its like
i dont deserve the kindness of others
the kindness ive been getting

as of lately.
its like
i stole & cheated
i lied & i fought
i ripped people off
the people closest to me too
& they didnt expect a thing....
not from me not from me
its like
what the fuck....

i bet
if i kicked you in the nuts
a cheap shot in broad daylight
hard & deep & solid
like a knife carving thru your fuckin nads
my boot rising as your testicles are
sucked inside you for your protection

you wudnt forgive me....

you wud hate me
you wud hate me
you wud hate me
until the day you died.

whats worst
i wudnt even cough up the dough
for your testicular surgery....

thats who i am

the twilight zone

& thats what i did
to everybody i touched.

jus punted them in the nuts.

yet they forgive me.
why?!

my sick kicks

my sick kicks....
walking down the street i want
my sick kicks.
& ill do—you bet ill do—
whatever i can to get
my sick kicks.

one of my earliest memories was
riding in the car w/ my mom
& we passed the newton highlands
train station where a mob of high schoolers
stood around smoking butts—*scum,*
my mom had spat, & drove away.

i remember watching them in their leather
w/ pierced ears & noses & the smoke—
oh how it coiled up from the stubs, it was
so amazing—& i vowed to live like that
some day one day eventually it wud happen
& i cud have

my sick kicks....

my sick kicks

(be one of the crowd)

(a part of the problem children
running amuck in this town)

walking w/ a limp ill get
my sick kicks.
children stare, parents sneer
but in the end its all the same
when i get my sick kicks.
my hairs a mess my face is dirty
my teeth are rotten & my hands
are filthy but none of that matters
because i got my sick kicks.

i learned early on that the crowd
wasnt all that its cracked up to be.
you got girls being catty & guys
they act all badass, machoism at its
very worst.... it was lame & i saw
right thru what it meant to be popular.

after all, they were way more
judgmental than even my own mom
whod spat scum & then drove off.
the cool kids were really deuchebags i
learned when i reached the ripe age
of when teenagers started trying to
get laid & the girls they knew this too.
they used this fact to get what they
wanted, but you see, all i wanted was

my sick kicks.

i know i know, i wanted sex like any
other high school kid but i wasnt willing
to play their games to get it because as i said
ive always got my hand to fall back on when
i need it & i cud have hollowed out
mount washington & stuffed it full of
all the tissues i used to clean up the messy
act of when your hand meets your—ill
stop right there & tell you this:

thank god for
my sick kicks.

i guess i cud say this nonchalant attitude
that i had did well in regards to getting
me laid because i got laid more than the
homophobic jocks who flush nerds heads
in the toilets for being a little too queer for
their school.

> "Jeremy gets more pussy than tampons,"
> a friend of mine once said.

but then that bored me.
sex bored me senseless.
they say if youre not having fun
then youre not doing it right.
ever met a kid who doesnt like pizza?
well, i guess hes not eating it right.

my sick kicks

i dreamed of gouging a girls eye out
w/ a spoon & stuffing my dick in there
to fuck her skull—before you cringe, think
of the metaphor there....
but of course no girl wud allow it
so i guess you cud say i prefer blowjobs
since its the closest i cud ever get to
an actual skullfuck.

even in porn id much rather watch
a girl blowing a dude than being stuffed by him.

theres a line in a song by
the forgotten rebels that goes:
who are you to judge morality?

all that crazy is is unconventional in a way.
i wanna fuck your brain & theres nothing
wrong with that unless you slap on the insanity
sticker & ship me off to the loony bin.

my clothing ripped, my face screwed up
in the most perfect scowl, permanently placed
to demonstrate the absolute disgust i feel
for modern day virtues, modern day values.
conventions can kiss my ass! cuz
ill do it my own way. these are my kicks & to you
they might seem sick
        very sick
        very fucking sick
        very fuck-fuck-fucking sick....

- 55 -

Jeremy Void

siiiiiiiiccckk
but you know what, to me

your kicks are sicker & fill me up with vile....
my sick kicks allow me to cope
            w/ all your conventional crap.

my sick kicks make me who i am
my sick kicks give my life a new meaning
my sick kicks arent really so sick
when seen under a certain light....

the world beneath me

there was a steady breeze coasting
past me as i crested the hill & reached
the peak of the mountain & peered outward
down at the world which swarmed w/ life.
life—boring, monotonous life, shimmering w/
neglect & it makes me restless....

d.i.y.

when i was a kid
i heard punk rock & i knew
i wanted to do it too.

as i got older & i read my first book
right then & there i knew
ive gotta write one too.

preachers

Nobody Knows Anything.
EVERYbody Is Doing The
Best They Can With The
Knowledge They Think They
KNOW.
humans by nature are ignorant.
we know nothing.
we pretend we know
but really we dont.

> then there are preachers.
> preachers are the worst.
> they feed you crap
> > about religion
> > about nutrition
> > about god &
> > progressive politics.

they know the least amount
of knowledge compensating by
forcing their own morals onto us
> onto me & you

& this must be stopped.

> conspiracy theories
> its all a conspiracy.
> im in the car after having
> conspired to drive down
> to quechie, vt.

take everything you hear
w/ a grain of salt.
what you see can be
deceiving & you shud not
believe it.
> faith is dead.
>> god is dead.

knowledge & facts rely
on faith
> in a scientist
> a *preacher*
> in somebody who cud very well be
> lying.................

idle poetry

sometimes my writing
has a mind of its own & it rises
from the page
swirling like a tornado of words,
gray & ghostly,
rising
higher higher higher,
& grasps the reader by his/her ears,
then stops spinning &
drops back into the page—
        a death-defying plunge, w/
        the reader in tow, delving
        deeper deeper deeper
        into the madness that is
        my writing

until

the reader is immersed
in my words....   HA!

no time

i wont let go.
im afraid time will pass me
too fast that ill be blinded
by its ongoing rush.
activities
events
flings
& the rest
i avoid so i dont get
swept up in the flurry
in the buzz
in the hustle
so that ill die
before ever having really been alive.
so i wont let go.

not in this lifetime...................

... i ...

i sit & wonder
i sit alone in the corner
i think of things i think of her
i think of the times we had
& i wonder how it all went bad.

am i the only guy in the world?
who feels this way, the only failure
of one thousand heads, one thousand
laughing faces smiling & happy
& mocking me to no end.

i hate myself i hate my life.
when i look at you its like
staring up at a giant, a big fat giant
rich & happy w/ a happy wife
& an even happier life
that reminds me ive got nothing & ill
always have nothing until i die.

i bite the tear-soaked barrel.
i bite it & i pray to something.

i ask to see the light before its too late.
i put pressure on the trigger which feels tight
in my grip, tight & hard & my last saving grace.

i hope you cry when i die
i hope your tears form a puddle on the ground
i hope you miss me & i hope ill never know
how much you cared...........

i hope i dont haveta live
to see a new day, i hope i can
work up the courage to finally do it
so for once i cud succeed in something

& i wont haveta die a failure.

untitled poem

when i raise my fist to the sky,
you better drop dead.
when i shout at the moon,
you better gimme all your money.
when i run, stomp, stagger, & spit,
you better leave me the fuck alone because
a knife is an ugly protrusion when its
jutting out of your back, all bloodied & gross.

a bang-up job

the only real car crash i remember getting into, for which i myself
was responsible, i was sober during—it took place after a court
date—i was 19-years old & being charged for possession of co-
caine—i got in a fight w/ my girlfriend over the phone—& one
thing led to another and:

i was speeding down the highway
in my purple minivan, staggering as
i drove in & outta cars. it was
reckless i know, only i didnt seem
to care, i was feeling rather
fuckin reckless at the time.
horns honked, i jus flipped them off.
i cut a sudden right & hit the offramp
that led to where i lived at the time, then
jerked the wheel left & cut over
the medium & rode up the on
ramp, cut a right & floored it
as i shot down the offramp like a kid
at a waterpark. i spun the wheel again
& hit the small field that ran alongside
the highway. i did crazy crazy crazy

donuts, kicking up dirt as i spun
round & round & round on the grass.
i combed the field as if crafting a
haphazard spiderweb then evened
myself out & mashed the gas pedal.
w/ an immediate jolt the van barreled
up the slope, faster faster faster
maxing out as i kept my foot hard on
the gas, & i ran right thru a small
bush—only it was not
a bush at all, it was a small tree w/
a rather thick trunk. the van slammed
right into the fuckin trunk, lifted up
as the airbag ejected, & came down
on its rear wheels, hard, & again, a
little less harder, the damaged shocks
catching its drop

—& then i climbed outta the
smoking van & lay down in the grass.
i guess some asshole called the cops,
thought i had been ejected from the
van itself. the cops gave me a hard time
when they found the stolen sludgehammer
in the backseat & the brown paper bag
w/ spraypaint residue packed into the
bottom—clearly for huffing—tucked away
in the glove compartment.

i admit i huffed, but not the day of.
i huffed the day before & forgot

it was in there. same w/ the sludge
hammer, which i grabbed from a
construction site while on my way from
a psychiatry appointment to my minivan,
parked somewhere in brookline, ma.

there were times when i drove drunk too, but for all those times i
suppose i got lucky: no crashes, no DUIs; jus luck. guess some-
thing so much greater than me had my back, or maybe it was in
fact jus good old-fashioned luck, i dont know. it cud have really
been anything when i think about it.…
i once backed out & hit a trashcan as i left a party, & then blacked
out for the remainder of the drive. i came to, finally, when i fell
thru the door & landed on my head. but i was home then anyway,
& i jus brushed myself off & staggered thru the front door & went
to bed. the next day when i went to visit my friend who had
thrown the party the night before i discovered that it wasnt a
trashcan that i had hit, it was a telephone pole.

the worst of my drunk driving probly happened when i went to
the dave & busters in providence, rhode island, w/ my girlfriend—
the two of us reached an alcohol-induced oblivion very quickly &
continued to push ourselves beyond oblivion until we breached
the realm of the absolutely retarded, complete & utter retarda-
tion; I mean, we got so *fuckin wasted*—since i had driven to pick
her up at her fathers house on the cape beforehand, & since she
had so much more experience w/ drunk driving than i did because
i only had my license for about 2 years at that point, she took the
wheel of my van & drove from providence, rhode island, to her
fathers house on the cape, w/ me along for the ride, sneaking
kisses every chance i cud get—we got to the cape & parked at the

a bang-up job

farm across the street from the condominium where her father
lives—we hooked up in the van for quite some time—& one thing
led to another and:

i found myself butt naked
behind the wheel of my van,
pressing the gas down hard w/
my bare foot & smoking a cigarette
w/ the window wide fuckin open,
& i mustve been so so cold since
it was winter then. i carelessly traversed
the highway, taking up all 4 lanes—
left & right across I95, wide staggers
that cud have killed somebody & myself.
luckily it was past 3 a.m. & the highway seemed
mostly deserted. i cant tell you how grateful i am
i didnt get pulled over that night. sitting
in the back of a cruiser butt naked & drunk
w/ a tiny dick as a result of the freezing
cold temperature wudve been quite the blow
to my already-low self-esteem. it wudve been
so humiliating & im so glad it didnt haveta happen
to me.

i think the best thing that did happen to me was when i wrapped
that van around the tree i thought was a little fern at first glance.
i totaled it all because i was angry & reckless, young & stupid &
looking for action, outta control & on the run from reality. i
crashed the van, destroyed it, fucked the shit out of it, hard hard
hard

& then, when it was all said & done, I had to pay my steep steep fines. for malicious destruction of property & reckless endangerment or something along those lines.

guess even good things come at a price.

a new poem

a new poem on a night
i have nothing to say—what
shud i say?
a new poem is such a fright
when the words dont come
as naturally as before. ohmygod,
theyre jus not flowing////
i wanna write something now but
i cant i cant i cant & this fact
is killing me, sir.
a new poem is deadly when it doesnt
pour our of your brain like chicken
noodle soup. gut pudding—yum yum yum.
maybe im hungry or im craving
caffeine. or something to set my mind
alight & something to ease the block
thats stabbing into my brain right now.

why wont somebody kill me please.

a photograph

i look at a photograph of me
my hair charged & black like charcoal
my eyes red like diamonds
my lips screwed up, cringing w/
      utter disgust
i see the resemblance, intellectually;
i can easily point out the similarities.
but if you ask me
     IF YOU ASK ME
who this man is, id tell you,
NOT ME   i dont feel this mans
aura, i dont feel a connection.
its like i stepped into a new dimension.

this man is lost, a victim of his own sick lust.
i was found, years ago, &
had evolved into something so much more
                than that.

        Sure, he & i are the same
        we share the same heart,
        only this mans heart—

a photograph

it was all mangled & gross
gutted & tangled, whereas my own
has been stitched back together. i feel like
a whole new person, & i dont seem to
recognize this image of the past anymore.

it seems so far-fetched to me.

enlightened

the lights come on, bright & brilliant
radiant

im in that state of mind when
my fingers are electric & they
thrum against the keyboard outta
my control. i do my best writing in this state
my best surreal landscapes. i lose
control of everything & my mind races.
my fingers, its like they shoot lightning bolts
from the tips that fill the computer screen w/
lines of words scrolling down the word document

i laugh at your writers block
really i do.
i had it once twice three times but now its gone.
its like ive become the master of my own domain.
they say you achieve that sensation from
masturbation, but me, i achieved it from
sleep-deprivation. fuck yeah, no sleep is where its
at if you wanna be as creative as one Jeremy Void.

enlightened

what do ive gotta say now to your puny absence
of control of your own life, of your own shell
of your own hell, deep & dark,
w/ dragons lurking in the fiery pits.

whipping & splashing, rising & falling,
w/ sharp, spiking waves, the lava that makes up your hell
snakes its way down the river trail. it undulates in
ferocious spurts that fold back into the lava as the fiery river
plows thru—you are

lost
disoriented
gone astray
obscured
& so fuckin inordinate that
its absurd to think that thats you, that
thats the life you live, jus the way
you are, cell upon cell stacked tight in a
roiling mass of ... huh ...

nothing?

but even so, amid the nothingness
that makes up your whole futile existence, you
stand proud—& i still dont get how you
pull it off—as life swirls & pounds in the background
like surround-sound speakers
or moreover, like a cage
the bars made of searing hot metal, red
& steamy, & you grab it

w/o first testing the temperature w/ your fingers—
you jus reach out & grasp it in your hand
& you dont feel a thing
        not even the predicted sting of heat that is
        guaranteed to tear you a new one when
        you get too close to it
well, not yet, at least

but what you do feel is completely unexpected
it feels like ice, so cold its like its putting you right to sleep
& your hand is numbing fast—

        wait for it … — … wait for it
        wait for it … — … wait for it
a rush of rising adrenaline growing all around you,
transforming into a vicious, manic beast, which gives
you cause enough to
panic—straight fuckin panic

then it comes to you like an electroshock
a sudden & startling realization that

THAT BAR IS FUCKING HOT!!!!

instantly you draw back your hand & see
the wisps of steam
streaming up from your singed fingers.

you hop around in agony, holding your burnt hand w/
a charcoal-black line like an indent running up your palm.
you hold it & scream, hopping & leaping about in

enlightened

utter fuckin torment—the pain is too strong & from all the
spastic jumping you inevitably bump your head on
the cages ceiling,
and

your lights go out
the best thing that cud have
ever happened to me

an eye opener

i was never really into denial
when i was a child, & i
never cared for lying as i grew
up to become the tall punk rocker that
i was
in those days.

life was simple:
question the truth because
anyone who knows anything
about anything
is so full of themselves.
w/ me included—especially
me.

i tried to tell the truth, never
leading anyone astray, & i
always tried to question au
thority so as to make certain we dont
lose
another one of our own. jus another teenager
dead for believing jus one more

an eye opener

fuckin lie, brought to you by
the teachers
the police
the state senators, going back as far as
the united states government

yeah, guess you cud call me
an anarchist. i was in fact against
the government & what they stood for.
i did in fact sneak into a veterans graveyard
& then later take pictures of my best friend
running down the street, holding up a
stolen american flag immersed in flames
trying to wave but dying in the licking flames
around it.

but
the thing is

i cudnt be an anarchist.
i was not self-righteous enough to stand for
a cause.
my convictions were lost in a
heaping pile of nothing that stood
so deep itd take a jackhammer to dig it out,
& that i did not have, because the jackhammer
id need cud very well make me blind.

but besides, to be an anarchist
one must believe they possess a certain knowledge
a certain knowledge which corrupts

a certain knowledge which brings small men
to their knees

& finally, a certain knowledge that is wrong
by definition!

shes the girl

it falls apart.
the whole world crumbles.
a girl sits amid the waste
waiting for her time to come.

shes tough
that girl, shes mean & she
doesnt have time enough
for luv. hate stands strong in
the culture she immersed herself in.
punk rock, spikes & black leather,
chains & snarling faces, & colored
hair.

she sits alone on the corner.
she sits & sips her 40-ounce of beer.
the passersby pretend to not stare,
but she senses the eyes of the normal,
beady & gross, zeroing in on her.
she flips them off & says, watchout
cuz ill eat your fuckin kids.

did she come from a broken home
was she molested, or was she jus smart,
too smart to fit into their mold. she
stands tall & says goodbye to the past,
kicking the future in the face w/
her heavy steel-toed doc martin boots.

her peers hate her, but thats okay.
her parents wanna change her, but
thats okay thats okay, cuz she doesnt
need their approval anyway. doesnt need their
lifestyle, its all so fuckin lame to her.

shes a tough punk rock chick.
shes nasty & shes sick. she has a razor blade
hanging from the chain around her neck.
her hair is green like snot, w/ an orange
like the color of rot stripe running down
the center of her head.
she wears a heavy biker jacket, in winter
or summer, studded & painted, like
a coat of armor.

when the band hits the stage,
shell be the first one dancing,
dancing w/ all the boys who swarm
& stagger & slam & crash into
one another. she swings her arms & gets
tossed from side to side, wavering about
in the mania all around her.

shes the girl

shes the girl all the most hardcore punks
wanna date, wanna take home & introduce
to their mom & pops.

shes tough & haggard, a real gem,
& she carries a fuck-off attitude around
her neck.

shes the girl im glad to have known.
shes the girl im glad to have
        taken home.
shes the girl that all the good little boys detest.
shes the girl that jus cant be arrested.
shes the girl….
        shes the girl….
                shes the girl
who died at 21 from a heavy overdose
        she hung herself
                she bled out in the bathtub
                        she was angry & hateful, a sad sad story
that never made the history books.
her life was wasted, dilapidated,
                but ill never forget that girl….

an art form

life is happening
& im dying.
or at least
i feel like im dying.
people—friends, family, neighbors
—all ebb, as i stand still.
i was the king of the hill
at one point in life
  (or at least
  thats how it felt
  to me, like i was a star
  like i was somebody
   anybody
  anybody but me at least),
but now the only stars i see
are the ones that blink out
in the sky, jus close their eyes &
go to sleep—disintegrating beauty.

i dont sleep anymore.
i stay awake all night & think
of things that make me depressed.

an art form

i tell people its to refresh those creative juices
i got boiling inside me because when i dont
sleep they boil over & spill out onto
the page.

im an artist. im lazy & weak.
im an artist, whose past was crazy
& whose future is bleak.
i wonder in vain why i didnt die
all those years ago, & i pray
oh how i pray
for that bullet to find my skull—
jus one stray bullet is all.

i know people will miss me,
        but i dont care.
now, whos the selfish one here?
i want to end my own misery
& they only want to prolong it.

surreal madness

the thump of the drums
as the drowning boy runs.
the crack of the knife
as it stabs thru your spine.

i stand at the edge of
the world watching the madness
echo & spray & ricochet
off the walls of my head.

the sound is so obnoxious.
the sound is so flamboyant.
a blast of noxious gasses
burning holes in the ozone layer.

i step off the cliff keeping one foot
grounded on the edge. i step & i dip
letting my foot hang there & then proceed
along the edge .... &
then i trip & fall...............

plummeting as

the drum racks
& slams
& smacks.
i clasp my hands together
& pray to the man above.
he stares down from the edge
& watches as i descend
into
madness.

the sea is bright blue.
the swans swoop & dive.
i swim & swim & flap
my wings as the water whooshes
past me.

its over now.
skidrow envelopes me.
im a bum
on the run .... from
myself.

stuck
fee fye fo fum
stuck
i smell the wrath
of my own fucking making ... of
my own fuck fuck fuck fuck fuck.

i run   i run   i run.
the wind spins & waves.

it hits my skin & im done for.

DUN DUN DUN….

the moral of **THIS** story

so

the lesson
the moral
the key piece of information
i want you to walk away w/
is:

whether it be drunk, angry, or jus plain naked
butt naked
in the end we all crash & burn (everyone)
        in the end…. so stop worrying
about it because your worrying
will only make us late….

high school riot (unfinished)

the kids are gathered around
united
& full of steam
picket signs gleaming
in the springtime heat.
a tall boy w/ dirty-blond hair
leads the pack, shouting chants
into the megaphone in his hand—
chants that are repeated by
the marching high school kids.

another day of school.
teachers stare down from their classrooms
out thru the windows, & watch
the concession of angst & rebellion
swirl beneath them.

no more, the tall, blond boy
barks, the call blasted thru the amp
in his hand.
no more, the teenagers say
manning picket signs &

waving them overhead.

the principal, a stocky man w/ an
obvious comb-over, waddles out
thru the front door. whats
the meaning of all this? he shouts.

no more, says the tall, blond boy
& a loud *no more* follows.
the principal pushes thru the march
reaches up & snatches a picket
sign from a brown-haired girl who shouts
hey! watchit!

a flame sparks, a wick ignited.
the flame climbs the thin piece of
string & the kid holding the cocktail
tosses it at the wall .... it
erupts w/ a splash of sparks.

the napalm glues the fire
to the bricks.
the flickering flames ascend the school.
the teachers gasp.
the principal hurries to the kid
responsible, grabs him by the throat
but .... a wooden plank-like
instrument is wrapped
around his head, hard, &
he goes straight
down like a manikin.

a riot starts.

a pandemonium of curses rise
from the flock of rioting kids.
they rush the school
windows explode amid the flurry.
the teachers hurry to the doors.
a youngish woman gets caught in
the flurry, her brown hair yanked
by a black-haired girl sporting a spikey
nose ring.
a balding science teacher is tackled by
a football player. a brown-haired math
teacher is beaten & bashed by a skater boy
the teachers face speckled w/ blood.

the fire alarm howls
the sound cutting & loud.
kids kick out windows,
knock over desks, loot loot loot
hooting as they go about smashing
the place up, tearing things
down down down...................

outside the principal rises
to his feet & retrieves his cellphone
from his inside pocket.

911, what seems to be the emergency?

these kids are

high school riot (unfinished)

out
of
control, he barks into the receiver.

hold, please.

he holds, not
given much choice
in the matter.

a voice comes on.
a man. stern. deep.
serious. *location, sir?*

the principal fills him in.
hangs up.
a window coughs up
a red fireball that flashes as it
latches on to the wall & starts its ascent.

ohmygod, he thinks.
what is going on?

sirens.

a cop car appears in
the distance.
an ambulance materializes
next followed by a firetruck bearing
down on the school, its massive, red
exterior bright & menacing in the

bleak world in & around the high
school.

sirens   sirens   sirens.
louder   louder   louder.
getting nearer   getting nearer
            getting nearer.

cop car #1 pulls to a stop.
the cop gets out as cop car #2
stops behind it. what the?
he mutters to himself gasping.

the firetrucks & the ambulances meet
the 3 cop cars on the scene.
men in red firemen suits pile out of
the firetrucks lined up before the
high school.

they stand there & watch for a moment then
retrieve hoses & go to work.
the cops retrieve riot guns that shoot beanbag
pellets & take aim on the kids they see
coming out the doors.

BANG BANG BANG as pellets zip
across the courtyard
& take down rioting kids.
BANG BANG BANG, more pellets
fly .... stunning the teenagers
running around in a haze of

high school riot (unfinished)

destruction.

kids drop.
pellets fly.
the fire dies as firemen
man the hoses that spray an
über powerful stream that
overrides the flames bursting thru windows
devouring the school in its fiery furry.

a mexican standoff (unfinished)

a boy & his father.
a mexican standoff.
the boy says, hey, daddy,
why wont you try this?
the daddy says, no no no
you better try this, sonny boy.

the boy holds out his hand
in which he holds a tab
of acid that cud really open
ones mind to that childish delight.

the father holds anti-
psychotics in his own hand
a mind-closing substance, a substance
to rob the child from the child.

no!
no, i will not take that my way
is the right way.
my way is good, why wont you be
more like me.

a mexican standoff (unfinished)

the boy cocks the hammer & raises
the pistol to point it at his pops.
the father does the same & aims
the gun at his own flesh & son.

they stand there, brows creased
& eyes gleaming w/ heat.
they are stern not about to
bend to the other ones whim,
not about to submit.

no fear shows in their eyes.
no remorse, because this means
war.

ok, the dad says after time
passes them by. ok, ill
try it if youll only try mine.

the boy ponders the deal
rehearsing the request in
his tiny boyish head.
ok, he replies. ok ok,
we/ll make a trade, then.
a tab of acid for
an anti-psychotic pill.

the dad smiles to hide his fear.
the boy smiles to hide his fear.
the two of them fear the
results of the submission to the
other ones whim.

www.ingramcontent.com/pod-product-compliance
Lightning Source LLC
Chambersburg PA
CBHW021205020426
42331CB00003B/211